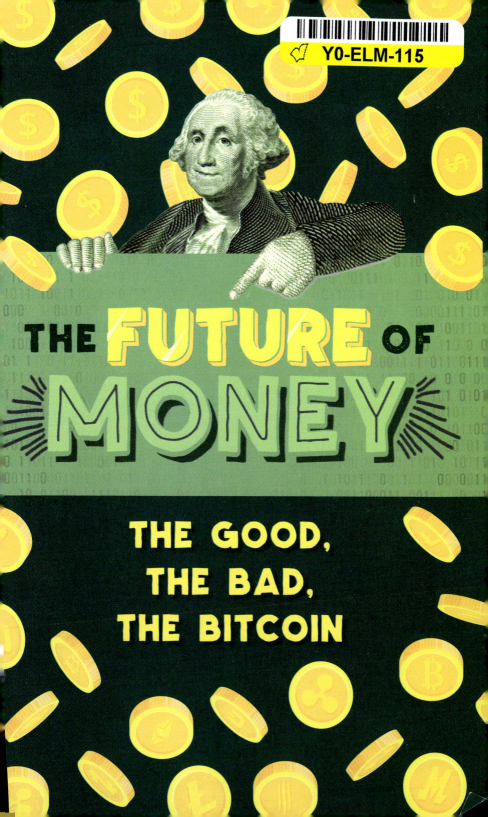

THE FUTURE OF MONEY

THE GOOD, THE BAD, THE BITCOIN

ISBN 978-1-338-33942-0

10 9 8 7 6 5 4 3 2   19 20 21 22 23

Printed in the U.S.A. 40
First printing 2019

Book design by Heather Kelly
Written by Elizabeth Milton

Photos ©: Alamy Images: 25 (www.BibleLandPictures.com); Shutterstock: 14 top (2018SENRYU), 34 left (alekseiveprev), 62 background (ananaline), 63 (Angel Dots), cover background (Anna Golant), 16 sacks (artmakerbit), 61 center (ASAG Studio), 46 center (Black or White), 18 cod (bonchan), 77 background (Borsuk Renat), 69 top (bsd), 32 background (chekart), 35 right (claptrap creatives), 31 clam (CloudyStock), 80 bottom (Denis Maliugin), 23 pudding (Dima Moroz), 41 (Dmytro Bochkov), 74 (DoozyDo), 18 tea (eAlisa), 7 museum (Eduard Radu), 20 (ekler), 28 (elbud), 77 top (Elena Abrazhevich), 9 beans (Elena Akimova), 39 top (estherpoon), 61 bottom (estherpoon), 17 background and throughout (Feryalsurel), 10 sand dollars (FishDesigns), 8 background (focus_bell), 43 background (Fotomay), 47 (Fox Design), 11 bottom right (Gal Istvan Gal), 14 bowls (GraphicsRF), 31 cabbage (HappyPictures), 25 arrows (Hollygraphic), 46 bottom (howcolour), 18 bottom right (Iakov Filimonov), 6 boy (Iconic Bestiary), 23 (Iconic Bestiary), 69 bottom (iconim), 72 (Ildarth), 30 (indigolotos), 35 left (Irina Strelnikova), 34 center (Jane Kelly), 35 center (Jane Kelly), 11 bottom left (johavel), 80 center (JR T), 70 top (Kakigori Studio), 60 bottom (Katy Flaty), 16 tree (Kazakova Maryia), 54 (Krafted), cover, 1 Washington (Lightspring), back cover Washington (Lightspring), 60 left (LineByLine), 57 (LuckyStep), 56 checkmark (LWY Partnership), 4 background (lyricsaima), 17 top left (Magdalena Paluchowska), 26 bottom right (Mark_Kostich), 6 shells (Martial Red), 61 top (Mary Long), 18, 19 chocolate bar (MarySan), 62 top (maximmmmum), 60 right (metamorworks), cover, 1 binary pattern (MicroOne), 55 (microtic), 71 bottom (Mihai Surdu), 31 deer (Mike McDonald), 39 bottom (Mikhail Mishchenko), 40 (Mikhail Mishchenko), 15 speech bubble (Milles Vector Studio), 9 coin (Mr. Rashad), 17, 19 shaker (mything), 18 beans (Nataly Studio), 11 top right (NikWB), 19 coins (NikWB), 29 (nimon), 11 top left (ogieurvil), 43 top (okasatriap), 53 coins (okasatriap), 18, 19 cod art (Olizabet), 8 cow (ONYXprj), 31 bread (Osman Vector), 24 top (pikepicture), 7 banner (PILart), 68 (Pogorelova Olga), 15 paperclip (ProStockStudio), 51 ledgers (Rashad Ashur), 11 center right (Ruslan_Grebeshkov), 19 bills (Ruslan_Grebeshkov), 19 top right (Sabelskaya), 45 (Sammby), 8 bill (Satanevich), cover spine (schab), 32 top (schab), 19 center right (Seashell World), 66 coins (Sensvector), 53 men and shield (Sentavio), 52 (ShadeDesign), 3 top (Shanvood), 4 top (Shanvood), 80 top (Sheila Fitzgerald), 26 penny (Spiroview Inc), 18, 19 tea bag (Spreadthesign), 21 (Stephen B. Goodwin), 10 piggy bank (Studio_G), 10 bill (Studio_G), 10 ice cream (Studio_G), 10 top right (Studio_G), 11 center left (Studio_G), 66 burst (studiostoks), 34 right (Succo Design), 5 (Sudowoodo), 60 top (Suiraton), 49 background (Suppachok N), 18, 19 camel art (Tarikdiz), 53 bottom (Tartila), 50 background (thitiwat_t1980), 17 bottom right (Tim UR), 65 (Titov Nikolai), 51 top right (Trikona), 14 man (tynyuk), 14 woman (tynyuk), 48 (Vadym Nechyporenko), 17, 19 bowl (Vasilyeva Larisa), 33 (vector toon), 24 background (Vector Tradition), 50 top (Venomous Vector), 58 (Viktorija Reuta), 16 top (Visual Generation), 78 (Visual Generation), 19 center left (Warren Price Photography), 51 top left (wasiliyg), 71 top (yellowline), 6 machine (Ysami), 31 bacon (Ysami), cover center bill (yum-yum), cover, 1 coins (Zefir), 70 bottom (Zoran Milic).

TABLE OF CONTENTS

INTRODUCTION

WHERE IS MONEY GOING?

Do you ever wonder what money will look like in the future—or if we will have money at all? Have you heard about cryptocurrency and want to know more about how it works? Are you wondering what in the world a blockchain is and what it is all about?

Before you learn about where money is headed, it might help to understand the basics . . .

LOL

Q: Where does money like to go on vacation?

A: To river banks!

BREAK OPEN THE PIGGY BANK...

What were your first experiences with money? Did you have a piggy bank or a special jar that you used to hold coins? Have you ever earned money by babysitting or shoveling snow in your neighborhood?

It might have felt strange the first time someone gave you money in exchange for your work or help. After all, if you were paid in dollar bills or coins, you were given what are basically pieces of paper and metal. Did you ever wonder what makes that money different from *regular* pieces of paper or metal? In other words, what makes money *money*?

SNACKS FOR SALE: FIVE SHELLS, PLEASE.

Now imagine if you used the money you earned to buy a snack from a vending machine. What if, instead of using coins or bills, you put *shells* into the coin slot? Believe it or not, before there was physical money, people used all kinds of things as payment, including actual shells!

While we don't use shells anymore, some people say that paper bills and metal coins might go away someday, too, if new payment methods continue to gain in popularity. If that happens, future generations—or even *you* in a few years—might think it's just as absurd to use paper or  metal to buy a snack as it would be to use a shell!

The changing shape of money is actually nothing new. Money has changed dramatically over the centuries, and it has never stopped evolving. Now you can pay for cabs or ride shares, food, and more just by tapping your phone! You don't even have to think about money changing hands because it happens behind the scenes between an app and your bank. There are even stores without cashiers or cash registers. They charge your account when you walk out with a product! A few years ago, this kind of technology would have only seemed possible in science fiction novels, but now it is becoming the new normal.

Cryptocurrency is another recent invention that is changing how people think about and define money. (What is it? You'll learn all about it later on!)

Cryptocurrency and new payment methods that let people send and receive money digitally are transforming how we make, send, and receive money.

WILL MONEY GO EXTINCT?

In some places in the world, such as Sweden and Kenya, the majority of financial transactions are already made digitally (such as on a smartphone, computer, or tablet) or using credit or debit cards. In Sweden, over a third of people report that they *never* use physical money—that's over 3 million people! It seems possible that physical money could go away completely in those countries—and maybe even the world. The question might not be *if* this will happen, but *when* . . . money might go the way of the dinosaurs and become a thing of the past.

CHAPTER 1

FROM COWS TO COCOA BEANS

Did you know that everything from cows (yes, actual cows!) to cocoa beans (used to make chocolate!) have been used as money? Strange as it might sound, it's true! And those are only a few things that have been used as money over the centuries.

Q: What do you call US dollars that you find in a vegetable garden?

A: Leafy greens.

WHAT IS MONEY?

To understand how cows, cocoa beans, and other things were used as money, and how money is changing, it helps to understand what money is and does.

Money is anything that can serve as a representation of value, but that's just the beginning!

There are three main functions of money:

1. A medium of exchange

2. A store of value

3. A unit of account

In short, money is anything that people can use to make purchases, that can be saved and used for later without losing its value, and that can help people determine the price to charge or pay for goods, services, and more.

So, what does it all mean? Here's a bit more about the three functions of money.

A MEDIUM OF EXCHANGE

Anything can be used as money as long as people agree that the chosen item is an acceptable way to exchange one thing for another. If you buy an ice-cream cone with dollar bills or with *sand* dollars, the act of being able to exchange one for the other is part of what makes something usable as money.

A STORE OF VALUE

This is also sometimes called a "measure" of value, but it's not the kind of measuring that's done with a ruler—it's more about the fact that money should stay at a similar value for a long time. This means that if you have 10 dollars and you put it in your piggy bank, in a few months those 10 dollars will hopefully still have a similar value or worth.

A UNIT OF ACCOUNT

This means that money can be used as the basis for prices. For example, if a pack of gum costs under a dollar, a laptop computer might cost hundreds of dollars, and a car might cost thousands of dollars.

In the same way, if oranges were being used as money in your society, people could decide that three orange slices would buy a pack of gum, and a wheelbarrow full of oranges might be enough to buy a new car. The fruit could be used both as a way to pay for things and a way to determine the price of things based on a number—or fraction—of oranges.

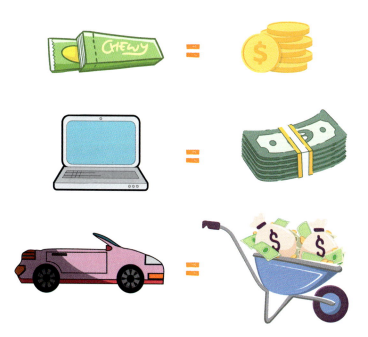

DOLLARS AND SENSE

So what makes something a good choice to be used as money? All of the reasons below help to explain why societies changed from using things like cocoa beans to using physical money created by a government, like metal coins and paper bills. That's because to work well, money needs to be:

1. **Divisible, or able to be divided into smaller units.** This is easy to do with a dollar, which can be exchanged for 4 quarters, or 10 dimes, or 100 pennies. It's even easy to divide an orange . . . but it's hard to divide a shell that is used as money!

2. **Portable, or easy to take places, even in larger quantities.** For example, if you have 1,000 dollars, it is easy to fit in a wallet in the form of ten 100-dollar bills, but if you use cows as money and have 1,000 cows, it would be very difficult to take them places!

3. **Acceptable, or able to be used as payment almost everywhere.** For example, US dollars are accepted as payment throughout the United States and can be exchanged for foreign currency when traveling.

4. **Scarce, or of limited supply.** If there are no limits on the supply of money, and either a too large amount

is printed by the government or people make fake money, the value of the money falls. In the United States, the central bank decides when to increase the supply of US dollars by printing more money, or to decrease the supply by taking existing money out of circulation. This helps the money hold on to its value. Another way to limit the supply is by making it difficult to make fake, or counterfeit, money. One way this is done is by adding security features that are hard to copy, like the color-shifting ink found on the US 20-dollar bill.

5. **Durable, or long-lasting.** For example, coins last a long time—around 25 years—because they are made of metal. This is good for many reasons, but mostly because it means they can be used for a long time without getting damaged. Bills are usually made on special paper that is designed to last as long as possible. The lifespan of a bill is actually more dependent on what it's worth! For example, a $1 bill only lasts around 5.8 years, compared to a $100 bill, which lasts around 15 years due to the fact that larger bills are used less frequently. One of the reasons corn wouldn't function well as money, on the other hand, is that it can rot in just a few days.

THE FUTURE OF MONEY BEGINS . . . WITH THE PAST

Before physical money existed in any form, people bartered, or traded, with other people to get the things they needed or wanted.

BARTERING

It might seem easy to barter or trade instead of needing money to purchase things or services, but it's not! Bartering works well when you exchange "like for like," such as if you grow carrots and you want peas. To barter

for something bigger, though, you might have to make a lot of trades and rely on people *wanting* what you have at each stage. It can get really complicated really fast. Even so, sometimes bartering pays off:

WHAT CAN YOU GET FOR ONE RED PAPER CLIP?

A man once tried a bartering experiment. He had one red paper clip and wanted to see what he could get for it. He offered the paper clip in exchange for . . . anything! First, he traded the red paper clip for a fish-shaped pen. He traded the pen for a handmade doorknob, which he traded for a camping stove, and eventually he was offered a small speaking role in a movie! After 14 trades in total, he was able to trade that movie role for a three-bedroom house in Canada! It's a great story, but it wouldn't have been such a success if no one wanted that red paper clip (or anything in between). Plus, it sounds like a lot of work!

COULD MONEY REALLY GROW ON TREES?

Bartering wasn't the only option in the past. Before there was physical money like metal coins or paper bills, civilizations used various objects—and even animals—as a form of payment. This is called "commodity money," because it gives another kind of value to items that already have a use or value on their own.

For example, those oranges we talked about earlier could be used as commodity money because they can both be used as a means of exchange (such as paying 10 oranges to go on a boat ride) and they can also can be eaten or made into juice. The seeds could even be used to grow a new orange tree to grow more oranges! In other words, if oranges were used as money, money really *would* grow on trees.

FUNNY MONEY

Here are some of the many amazing things people have used as money over the centuries.

SPICES

SALT

In the Middle Ages, East Africa used salt as a medium of exchange. Its use as a currency was most widespread in Ethiopia, where it was used until the mid-20th century. Salt was mixed with wood chips to help protect it, molded into rectangular blocks, and wrapped in straw. These bars of salt were called "amoles" after the Amole tribe that first used it.

Salt was also used as money in the Roman Empire and in ancient Britain. Salt was even part of the payment given to Roman soldiers, which was called a "salarium." It is the root of the words "salary" and "salad," because they used the salt on their greens!

PEPPERCORNS

Peppercorns—the small dried berries that are ground into pepper to season food—were once considered so valuable that they were accepted as a form of payment.

In the year 410, a man known as "the Barbarian," or Alaric, went to the gates of Rome and demanded a ransom of gold, silver, and other valuables, and 3,000 pounds of peppercorns—and the Romans paid it.

In the Middle Ages in ancient Britain, peppercorns were used as money, too, for everything from rent to taxes.

BEANS AND LEAVES

TEA BRICKS

Tea leaves that were ground up and then molded into small squares or rectangles called "tea bricks"—often with beautiful designs on them—were used as money in Tibet, China, Mongolia, and Siberia.

COCOA BEANS

Aztecs used cocoa beans—the beans used to make chocolate bars and hot chocolate—as money. Who knew money could be so sweet and tasty?

FISH AND LIVESTOCK

CODFISH

In the mid-1600s in Newfoundland, dried cod was accepted as payment. Now, that's fishy . . . literally!

COWS, CAMELS, AND SHEEP

Between 9000 and 6000 BC, cows, camels, and sheep were used as money!

SHELLS AND BEADS

COWRIE SHELLS

Cowrie shells—the shell of a kind of sea snail or mollusk—are the longest-used currency and were used in China, India, Thailand, Vietnam, the Philippines, the Maldives, New Guinea, and Africa for centuries. In China, they were used at least since 1600 BC and were the inspiration for the first Chinese character for money (which looked like a cowrie shell).

WAMPUM BEADS

Native American tribes used strings of white beads made from clamshells—called "wampum beads"—as money. From 1637 to 1661, wampum was also a legal form of money in New England. This is where the term "shelling out" money originated . . . from places where people literally pulled shells from their pockets to pay for goods!

STONE MONEY

The island of Yap, in the Pacific Ocean, has a unique form of money called the "rai." It was first created hundreds of years ago when people from Yap found an island hundreds of miles away with a lot of limestone. They mined the limestone and carved it into giant discs, each with a hole in the center, and then loaded the discs onto their boats and sailed back to Yap with the discs. The discs were considered valuable, and were eventually used as money even though they are enormous. A rai can be as large as 12 feet in diameter and 8,000 pounds, weighing more than a car!

Luckily, people don't have to move the stones to use them as money. They just make sure to discuss who owns it, using a verbal agreement, once a transaction has been made. They are still used today as commemorative tokens for special occasions, in addition to a more useable—and portable—currency.

The system is unique for a lot of reasons, but one in particular. Legend has it that one time, a sailor was returning to Yap from the island with the limestone and hit rough waters, and a rai fell into the ocean. When the sailor returned to Yap and shared the story, the people of Yap decided that the stone money was still valuable even though it was on the ocean floor, and that it could still belong to its owner! Someone on Yap still owns that rai, even though it has been at the bottom of the ocean for a century!

Wouldn't it be amazing if you had some money, dropped it in the ocean, and could still use it to buy whatever you wanted?

A 32-CENT STAMP PRINTED IN THE FEDERATED STATES OF MICRONESIA AROUND 1996, SHOWING RAI, THE STONE MONEY.

WHAT ELSE COULD BE USED AS MONEY? HINT: IT'S DELICIOUS . . .

All of those items used as money might seem really different from one another, but they have something in common: they were used as money because they were highly valued.

Can you imagine something in your world that you value . . . and could use as money if you didn't have printed money or coins? It might help to narrow it down to a category, like food, and think about a kind of food you value.

For example, when you bring lunch to school, have you ever traded parts of it for a friend's chocolate pudding cup? If you and your friends value pudding cups, you could use pudding cups as payment just like we use coins today and just like people used peppercorns in the past! How many pudding cups do you think it would cost to buy a bag of carrot sticks, or a pencil, or a backpack? How about a car or a plane ticket?

Other things that can be used as money are less yummy and more useful, such as toilet paper rolls. It may seem silly, but if physical money didn't exist anymore, toilet paper might be valuable enough to use as money!

CHAPTER 2

CASH, COINS, DOLLARS, AND DOUGH

THE FIRST COINS

While metallic money was used in 2000 BCE in Babylon, according to a recent discovery, the first coins were made out of bronze in 1000 BCE in China. Historians also consider coins made in the 7th century BCE in the ancient kingdom of Lydia (what is now Turkey) to be some of the first coins ever used. These coins were made out of a mixture of gold and silver metals called "elec-

LOL

Q: What would babies value enough to use as money?

A: A diaper change!

trum." The coins were bean-shaped and had a design on one side and punches on the other. It was hard to tell the different coins apart, so historians believe they were often weighed instead of counted.

THE FIRST PAPER MONEY, OR "FLYING MONEY"

China was the first country to use paper bills, in the 7th century. Before that, they had used copper coins, but big bags of coins were very heavy to carry around, especially if people needed to carry large amounts of money. Eventually, merchants decided to create paper certificates to carry around instead of the coins. These certificates were nicknamed "flying money" because they tended to blow away in the wind.

SILVER COINS DISCOVERED IN THE ANCIENT KINGDOM OF LYDIA AROUND 561-546 BCE

THINGS YOU MIGHT NOT KNOW ABOUT US CURRENCY

Rumor has it that Martha Washington donated her silverware to make the first US coins and that she may even be pictured on them. Other records suggest that Thomas Jefferson may have paid for the silver for the coins instead. We may never know for sure, but one thing is certain, those first coins are very, very valuable today. Valued at five cents in 1792, they have sold for up to 2 million dollars. Here are some more cool and curious things you might not know about US currency.

PENNIES

- The first one-cent piece was so large—almost as big as a half-dollar coin—that it is now referred to as the "large cent." It was used from 1793 to 1857. Depending on the condition and rarity, today these coins can be worth up to thousands of dollars!

- "Silly heads" were the nickname for large cents that were minted in 1839. These coins featured a portrait of Lady Liberty that many thought looked silly! They are now worth around $27 apiece, or up to $1,206 for a coin that was never in circulation. A very rare one once sold for $4,465.

- In 1943, the copper used to make pennies was needed for World War II, so pennies were made out of zinc-coated steel.

ONE OF THE FIRST US COINS NEXT TO A PRESENT DAY PENNY.

NICKELS

- Five-cent coins are called "nickels" because they were usually made of nickel, a kind of metal. For a short period of time, during World War II, when the metal nickel was needed, nickels contained no nickel at all.

- The word "nickel" actually comes from the German word *kupfernickel*, meaning "false copper," also translated as "rascal." This is because nickel ore, or the way the metal appears when mined, is easily mistaken for copper ore, which is more valuable. People sometimes thought they had struck it rich by finding copper ore—until they realized it was just nickel, that rascal metal that looked like copper!

- In 1953, a Brooklyn newspaper boy was paid with a nickel that felt lighter than usual. He dropped it, and the nickel popped open . . . and it was *hollow* inside. In the hollow space, he found a tiny photograph with numbers on it. The coin was eventually given to the Federal Bureau of Investigation. The nickel was one of many hollowed-out objects that Russian spies used to share coded messages.

DIMES

- Dimes and other larger US coins have grooves on the edges. These were added when the coins were made of gold and silver to keep people from filing the edges of the coins to get some of the precious metals.

- In the early 1900s, a shipment of dimes intended for the San Francisco Mint apparently fell off a cliff in Utah . . . and has never been found.

QUARTERS

- These 25-cent pieces were the first US coins to have a number on them to denote their value. The number was added in 1804. Until then, people had to know the value of coins based on their size.

HALF-DOLLAR COINS

- The half dollar was the first coin to feature an African American. It was the Booker T. Washington Memorial Half-Dollar, minted from 1946 to 1951. They are now worth from around $14 to $115.

DOLLAR COINS

- The word "dollar" comes from a German word for a large silver coin called a *thaler*.

- In the late 1800s and early 1900s, silver dollars had a fun nickname. People called them "cartwheels" in part because stars were arranged around the edge of the coins in a way that reminded people of the notches on wooden wheels used on carts and wagons. It may also have been because they were larger and heavier than other coins, or as big as the wheel of a cart, at least compared to smaller coins. These can be worth anywhere from around 18 dollars to hundreds of thousands of dollars today, depending on the condition and rarity.

DOLLAR BILLS

GENERAL FACTS ABOUT US DOLLARS

- United States dollars are printed on paper that is actually not paper at all. Paper is usually made of wood pulp. US dollars are 75 percent cotton and 25 percent linen. That's why, if you wash a bill by mistake, it will usually survive (but do not try this at home, just in case)!

- If you look really closely, the paper used to make US dollars has red and blue fibers inside it. This is meant to make it more difficult to produce fakes.

- From the 1800s to the 1990s, 30 percent of the cotton in the paper used to make US dollars actually came from denim fabric scraps from clothing manufacturers who made things like jeans! This ended because clothing designers started adding spandex to denim material to make jeans stretchy.

$1 BILL

- The design of the $1 bill has been the same since 1963. Designs for larger bills change more often, in part because people who try to make fake money (which is a crime) tend to not try to fake a $1 bill since its value is relatively low.

$2 BILL

- Have you ever seen a $2 bill in person? When people get $2 bills, they tend to keep them as collector's items instead of spending them, so they seem rare even though they aren't. One reason for this may be that some people *think* they are so rare that they could potentially be valued at more than $2.

- One superstition related to the $2 bill is that if you give one to a traveler before on a journey, it will bring them good luck and make it more likely that they will return the money to you.

- Some US Air Force pilots carry $2 bills in their flight suits. It's because they fly a special aircraft called a U-2 spy plane. They even try to match the $2 bill's serial number to the last few digits of their pilot identification number.

LARGER BILLS

Nowadays, the largest dollar bill is the $100 bill, but there have been much, much larger bills for $500, $1,000, $5,000, and even $10,000. These were discontinued in 1969 because, understandably, they weren't used by a lot of people.

DOUGH, BREAD, BUCKS, AND OTHER SLANG WORDS FOR MONEY

Did you know that there are all kinds of slang words for money? An artist named Mel Bochner even made a painting filled solely with slang words for money painted in bright colors!

Here are just a few of the words people have used over the years in place of "coins," "money," "cash," and more.

BACON: This slang word is usually used in the context of money earned through working, as in, "bringing home the bacon."

BREAD and related words like **DOUGH**: These slang words came about because of the idea that bread—like money—was needed to stay alive since it was a main source of food. It is also the root of the word "breadwinner," which refers to a person who is the primary earner for him or herself and a family or household.

BUCKS: Possibly comes from the 19th-century American frontier and the habit of using buckskins as money.

CABBAGE and related words like **LETTUCE**: Rumor has it that this slang came about because these vegetables are a similar green to the color of dollar bills.

CLAMS: Saying one clam instead of one dollar apparently comes from the history of using clamshells as currency.

CHAPTER 3

DIGITAL DOLLARS:

FROM DIGITAL PAYMENTS TO MOBILE MONEY

What would happen if you wanted to buy an ice-cream cone and you left your money at home? You probably wouldn't get to have ice cream unless someone else bought it for you.

Q: What did the baker use as Monopoly money?

A: Play-dough.

In the future, some people think physical money (like bills and coins) and even plastic credit cards might go away completely and be replaced with digital payment methods, like paying using a smartphone. If this happens, anyone could leave the house without their wallet . . . and still be able to purchase anything and everything! Already, only two percent of financial transactions are made with coins and bills. Ninety-eight percent are made using credit cards, mobile banking, and other payment methods.

HOW DID WE GET HERE?

A variety of different payment methods and technologies paved the way for digital payments and mobile money.

DIGITAL DOLLARS THROUGH TIME

CREDIT CARDS

Soon, more cards similar to the Diners Club Card followed and eventually led to modern-day credit cards. They allowed people to buy items without cash—by basically borrowing money—and pay for them later. The downside, though, is that if people spend more than what they can afford to pay when their bill is due, or if they forget to pay their bill, they are charged extra.

9TH-CENTURY PERSIA

1950

1959

CHECKS

Early versions of checks were used many hundreds of years ago. The version most similar to modern checks was used in 9th-century Persia. The word "check" is said to come from the Persian word *sakk*, which was a piece of paper that people could use as a substitute for money so they wouldn't have to carry heavy coins when they traveled. In fact, a check could be handwritten on any piece of paper up until 1762, when a British banker named Lawrence Childs invented the printed check. While checks are being used less and less, they are still a way of paying with money without money actually changing hands.

DINERS CLUB CARD

This is often considered to be the first credit card. The idea came about because a businessman named Frank McNamara went out for dinner, and realized he forgot his wallet. In those days, cash or checks were the only option for payment. He was so embarrassed that he couldn't pay the bill—even though his wife had cash and paid for it right away—he started a club that would let diners pay using a membership card, and then be billed at the end of the month for all of their purchases.

ONLINE BANKING

When online banking became available, even more financial services could be accessed from home—or anywhere in the world, as long as there was an internet connection!

Years later, another innovation was created by a company called Square: a small card reader that could be plugged into the headphone jack of a smartphone. This allowed small businesses—and even places like farmers markets that used to only take cash—to accept credit card payments more easily than with a standard machine.

PAYPAL

1967   **1981**   **1999**   **2009**

ATMS

ATM stands for Automated Teller Machine. A "teller" is a person who works behind the front counter of a bank who handles daily transactions such as cash withdrawals and depositing checks. With the invention of ATMs, people were able to withdraw cash and deposit checks after the bank's operating hours for the first time.

PAYPAL

As people began to shop online, they needed a way to pay for the purchases they were making with less risk of hackers getting their credit card or bank account information. PayPal helped people pay more safely from home.

"INVISIBLE" MONEY

One of the reasons money seems invisible is because there are so many ways people can pay using a mobile phone or other devices. That's not as new an idea as you might think. Believe it or not, Coca-Cola was the first company to accept payments by mobile phone. Back in 1997, they allowed people to buy Coca-Cola at special vending machines and pay for the drinks by sending a text message!

Technology has come a long way since then, and now people can pay for almost anything using a smartphone.

Near-field communication lets people tap their phone near a card reader to make a payment.

Mobile wallets let people store credit card and other payment information on their phones so they don't have to take out their wallets to pay.

Person-to-person payment methods like Venmo, Square Cash, and Google Pay make it much easier to pay individuals. Instead of needing exact cash or a check to pay someone back for a portion of the bill at a restaurant, for example, people can pay using their phones.

Someday these technologies, and ones that haven't been invented yet, might even make wallets a thing of the past. Maybe people will collect wallets like they collect antiques!

Here are just a few new technologies that are already being used or tested and make money practically invisible.

WEARABLES

Wearables are things like bracelets or rings equipped with technology that lets you pay with a swipe of your wrist or finger when you wear them.

You can already pay with a smartwatch, too. Maybe someday you will be able to pay with your favorite necklace or your glasses!

BIOMETRICS

Another futuristic technology that makes mobile payments possible uses what is called "biometrics." The word includes "bio," which means "life," and "metrics" which means "measuring." It involves scanning a part of a person's body—such as their fingerprint, eye, or the palm of their hand—and comparing that scan to one in a database to make sure the measurements and other characteristics match.

Biometric technology is already used on phones that have fingerprint scanners, and also on some security systems.

Did you know you can pay with your *face*? Face ID

uses facial recognition software and a phone's self-facing camera (the one used for selfies) to confirm your identity so you can access payment information on your phone.

Another version of this technology that is already being tested might let you pay by simply holding your hand over a scanner. It involves a sensor that actually looks at the vein patterns in your hand and compares them with patterns of an image it has on file to make sure the patterns match and to confirm that you are who you say you are.

Maybe one day you will pay just by saying "pay" out loud! Biometric technology can already recognize voices . . . but this idea would only work if the tech couldn't be fooled by a voice recording!

OH MY, MICROCHIPS!

One other version of this might go a little too far . . . by letting people use an implanted microchip in their hand to pay for things like train tickets or even snacks at their office. It seems easier to just pay the old-fashioned way!

Who knows . . . maybe someday you'll be able to pay with a glance of your eyeball, or even just by *thinking* about it!

WHY ARE MOBILE PAYMENT METHODS GROWING?

SPEED: It can be faster than paying by cash or even by credit card.

SECURITY: With fingerprint scanners and other technology to verify a person's identity, these digital payment systems could be more secure.

SAFETY: Some businesses are even going cash-free and only accepting digital payment methods. This is considered to be safer for employees who might be at risk of robberies if they have a lot of cash on hand from daily transactions.

MORE SANITARY: Cash is crawling with germs! Studies show that a dollar bill can have 3,000 types of bacteria on its surface—that's dirtier than a toilet! With fewer cash transactions, it is possible that germs aren't as likely to be passed between people.

ALMOST CASHLESS: AROUND THE WORLD

This is already becoming a reality in places like Sweden and Kenya, which are already almost entirely cashless societies.

SWISH IN SWEDEN

In Sweden, the most popular payment app is called Swish. It is so widely used that cash is becoming a rarity. Many banks don't even have cash on hand anymore! Swedes can use the credit cards or payment apps to pay for everything from bus rides to small purchases like packs of gum, and many churches and even street vendors accept Swish!

M-PESA IN KENYA

In Kenya, the most popular payment app is called M-Pesa, named after the Swahili word for money, the pesa. The app was created by the country's biggest mobile phone service provider, called Safaricom, and it launched in 2007. It was started, in part, because people in rural parts of the country didn't have easy access to banks. The app allowed them to pay for things digitally, even if they didn't have cash.

ON THE WAY TO CASHLESS? GETTING RID OF LARGE BILLS

Many countries, including France, the UK, and India, are taking the largest bills out of circulation. It's both a way to encourage people to pay with credit cards or digital payment methods and to discourage crime. People say it could be a step toward a cashless society.

THE GOOD, THE BAD, AND THE CASHLESS SOCIETY

In the future, physical money may not exist at all, but it's hard to know when or if something like this will happen. It's also hard to know if it will be a good thing, a bad thing, or something in between. Whether cryptocurrency, mobile payments, or some other technology becomes the preferred payment method, a future without cash has a variety of advantages and disadvantages worth exploring.

Some of the many reasons people are already using mobile payment methods—like the convenience, speed of transactions, and ability to pay without having to carry anything other than a smartphone—are the same reasons a cashless world might be a safer, more efficient, and more peaceful world. A cashless society could make it harder for people to commit crimes—or even discourage them from doing so—because all purchases would be trackable. It could also make it easier to catch mistakes in orders or record keeping, and maybe even make it almost impossible to counterfeit money.

However, going completely cashless could ultimately be bad for businesses, especially small businesses like locally owned stores. Every time a purchase is made with a credit card, the credit card company takes a percentage of the payment as its fee. Over time, those fees can add up and directly impact a small business's profits.

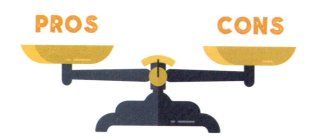

One disadvantage of digital money and credit cards that isn't as easily seen is their dependence on electricity to function. If you rely on your phone to make payments and the battery dies, you'd be out of luck until you charge your phone. On a larger scale, if the power ever goes out, it would be impossible to use a credit card or other digital payment method.

- If one store lost power for a day due to technical problems, then they have lost an entire day's worth of profits.

- If the power in an entire city goes out after a natural disaster, there would be no way to pay for food, gas, water, or other essentials without the use of cash.

- Perhaps worst of all, a transition to a cashless society would be particularly difficult for someone who does not have access to technology or the ability to open a bank or credit card account.

CHAPTER 4

DECRYPTING CRYPTOCURRENCY

Cryptocurrency could be the next frontier for the future of money. You might know much about cryptocurrency, or maybe you have heard the word but don't really know much else about it.

Before we get into the details, have you ever wondered why people wanted a new form of currency? Or have you wondered why people may not be happy to just use cash, credit cards, or one of the many other payment methods available? These issues are just some of the reasons cryptocurrency was created.

LOL

Q: What's a nice price for a bottle of perfume?

A: Twenty dollars and fifty scents.

THE NEED FOR TRUST

When we buy things online, every transaction we make—such as buying a toothbrush or a book, or paying for a movie streaming service—has to go through a bank or credit card company. These companies keep records of all payments, purchases, deposits, and other transactions in client's accounts. They are the sole, or only, record keepers, and that makes some people nervous that the records might not always be correct. People are also concerned about how to keep their information secure during online purchases. The lack of trust and concerns about privacy are a few of the reasons people want cryptocurrency.

THE DATA DILEMMA

Many people don't like the fact that online activity is tracked. Whether a person is browsing the internet, engaging in social media, or making online purchases, many websites track habits, interests, online searches, and more information. Those companies can then use that data, or information, to sell to other companies or to sell advertisements.

Imagine if every time you bought lunch from the school cafeteria, your school was keeping track of you, what you bought, when you bought it, and what that might say about you. Then, what if your school was selling the information it collected about you and all of your classmates to a local park so the park could sell food you and your classmates enjoy? This might not sound like such a bad thing, but it could feel a little creepy.

Another example would be if you shopped for a video game online, and the website you were visiting collected or tracked your shopping and browsing data. Then, if you randomly checked the weather on another website, you might see an ad for those video games.

These experiences might be harmless, but some people don't like that companies know and track their habits, even something as simple as shopping. Some people are worried this information could be hacked by people looking for sensitive information—like credit card numbers. People also worry that there are ways all this information could be used against them in the future in ways they don't yet know or understand. When online companies sell the information they collect they are making a profit off your everyday actions and choices.

WHAT IS CRYPTOCURRENCY?

Because of these issues and others, some people wanted to create a new kind of currency that could be used online in the same way cash can be used in person. Cash is difficult to track, which means it can be used with fewer restrictions and without the widespread privacy issues of the internet. Aside from the fact that it functions a bit like cash, cryptocurrency is different from regular money in almost every way.

The main ways cryptocurrency is different from other currency is that it is:

1. **DIGITAL**—It does not exist in any physical form like a coin or bill. Cryptocurrency is both created and stored electronically.

2. **DECENTRALIZED**—It is not controlled by a central government or authority, although this is not always the case. Instead, it is usually controlled by peer-to-peer networks of computers (we'll explain in more detail later!).

3. ENCRYPTED—The information is concealed in a secret code. A code is basically a language that can only be translated using a secret password or key. This makes it difficult to create fake, or counterfeit, cryptocurrency, and also provides a way to securely transfer funds.

PUTTING THE "CRYPTO" IN CRYPTOCURRENCY

The "crypto" in cryptocurrency comes from the word "crypt," which means "hidden" or "secret." It is also the first part of the word "cryptography," which is a way to transform text (such as by using a secret code) to conceal its true meaning so that only the intended recipient can read or understand it. Information that has been changed from one form to another using cryptography is called "encrypted" information.

Cryptography is nothing new—in fact, the first use of some form of cryptography is thought to be from about 1900 BC! Cryptography is probably most well known for being used by spies as a way to pass secret messages. It is also used behind the scenes to protect all kinds of sensitive data, like passwords for websites and credit card information.

Cryptography is arguably one of the most important parts of cryptocurrency because it's what helps cryptocurrency hold its value. Most currencies today aren't based on the value of a physical item or commodity like they once were. The US dollar was once based on gold because gold was rare. Now it is backed by the government instead of gold, and holds its value by being hard to reproduce. That's why some bills have security ribbons woven into the paper, security threads that glow when held under an ultraviolet lightbulb, color-shifting ink, raised printing that gives the bills a unique texture, and more. Cryptocurrency accomplishes the same kind—or possibly even better—security in a different way, by being protected by cryptography.

CAN YOU CRACK THE CODE?

Now it's your turn to try to decode a secret message like a cryptographer! In the code below, every letter in the alphabet corresponds to the letter underneath. For example, if you were writing "HI, MOM!" using the code, it would look like "IJ, NMN!"

See if you can decode the following secret message!

Alphabet: A B C D E F G H I J K L M N O P Q R S T U V W X Y Z
Code: B C D E F G H I J K L M N O P Q R S T U V W X Y Z A

Encrypted message:
DSZQUPHSBQIZ JT BO JNQPSUBOU QBSU
PG DSZQUPDVSSFODZ.

_ _
_ _ _ _ _ _ _ _ _ _ _ _ _ _ _.

This activity is one simple way that coding, cryptography, and encryption work together to protect information. When you are done, check the answer key below to see how you did!

Up for a challenge? Try writing a note to a friend or sibling and give them the code above so they can read your secret message. Up for a bigger challenge? Create your own code to encrypt messages by using a different arrangement of the alphabet, emojis, or random symbols in place of letters!

CHAPTER 5

BUT FIRST . . . BLOCKCHAIN

Blockchain technology is what makes it possible to have money, like Bitcoin or other cryptocurrencies, that is not controlled by a central government or authority. It does this by keeping track of every transaction as a kind of ledger, or record of financial activity.

WHAT IS IT?

Blockchain is a database that stores records or information. It is called blockchain because it is a chain of connected blocks of information.

LOL

Q: What kind of cat should you never trust with your money?

A: A cheetah!

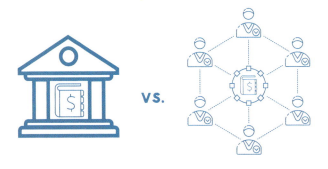

BLOCKCHAIN, IN BRIEF

Traditional ledgers are books or lists used to record financial transactions in an account. These ledgers are usually controlled by one person or company, such as a bank.

A DISTRIBUTED LEDGER

Blockchain is different because its information is stored on a network of computers that work together to verify the information of each transaction. This is called a *distributed* ledger. Instead of recording transactions in one central ledger, its information is distributed to many different computers. They keep track of each Bitcoin and who owns it, and verify that it is authentic.

Anyone can use the blockchain, and everyone who uses it holds a copy of the *entire* ledger on their computer. Better yet, all of the users record each transaction on their computers at the same time. The advantage of this is that anytime a change is made, all the other computers in the blockchain network are checked to make sure that the change is accurate.

51

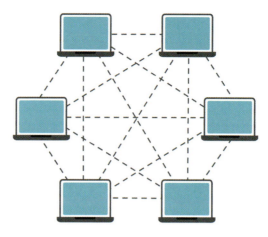

PEER-TO-PEER NETWORKS AND NODES

Blockchain is actually a technique of documenting information with a high level of security, and it was first described in 1991 by a team of researchers who said it could be used to prevent tampering with digital documents by giving them a kind of "timestamp," or marking them with the date and time they were created.

The blockchain network is called a peer-to-peer network because it is made up of so many different computers. Whenever someone joins it, they get a full copy of the blockchain on their computer or hard drive, which becomes a "node" in the network. Nodes are computers connected to the blockchain network. When a new block is created, each node checks to make sure that the block is valid. If all of the nodes in the network agree, then the block is added to the chain.

SECURITY, BLOCKCHAIN-STYLE!

This network of personal computers holding data is one of the things that makes blockchain more secure and also more trustworthy than traditional ledgers. Since there are so many copies, it is very difficult for one person to hack, corrupt, or misuse. If they try,  the other computers involved each hold a backup of all of the information and can prove that some information was changed.

Think of it this way: If you had a homework assignment that was stored digitally, and you were the only one able to make changes to it, you could easily change it. But imagine if a copy of your homework was stored on the computer of everyone in your school. Now imagine that every time you answered another question in the assignment, all of those computers made sure the

only change made was only to the latest question. This constant checking would make it very difficult to make a change to the complete document. Anyone with a copy of your assignment would have proof of how it used to be.

PROOF-OF-WORK

To keep hackers from programming computers to just changing the code, the blockchain has a safety measure called a "proof-of-work" that slows the creation of new blocks. Bitcoin, for example, takes ten minutes to calculate the proof-of-work once a change has been made to a block. If someone tries to change one of the blocks, they'll also need to devote ten minutes per block to recalculate the proof-of-work for each block that follows in the chain. This may not seem too bad, but if you multiply it by the number of Bitcoins—currently around 17 million—it could take a very, very long time!

HOW DOES THE BLOCKCHAIN WORK?

STEP 1:
A RECORD IS CREATED.

If you decided to buy a fraction of a Bitcoin from a friend, a record of that transaction would be kept in the blockchain—including details of the purchase and a digital signature from both you and your friend. The digital signature isn't a signature at all; it's actually a string of numbers created using cryptography.

It might be easier to think of in another way, like if you were buying cookies. If instead of buying Bitcoin you were buying a cookie at a bake sale, this first step would be making a record of the details of your cookie purchase, like a receipt. Except *everyone* at the bake sale would be responsible for recording the information, including you. Let's say you all have a piece of paper that lists all sales from the bake sale. The record would also include a signature from both you and the person selling cookies.

STEP 2:
THE NETWORK CHECKS THE RECORD TO MAKE SURE IT IS VALID.

Every computer belonging to anyone who owns Bitcoin, in this case, becomes part of the network that verifies the records of future transactions. Each computer is called a "node" in the network. For a new record to be accepted, each individual node—or computer—must check the details of the purchase to make sure the new record is the *only* thing that has changed during the transaction.

Let's continue to think of this in terms of cookies. This would be like every person at the bake sale was confirming how much you paid, what you bought, and whether or not you and the seller are actually the ones making the exchange. If everything matches, your purchase is officially added to everyone's notebooks (including your own)—this is the ledger in Bitcoin. If there is something on one person's page that doesn't match everyone else's pages, your sale would not go through and you wouldn't get your cookie.

STEP 3:
THE NEW RECORD IS
ADDED TO A BLOCK.

The record of the deal you made is grouped together with other records to form a larger block.

In cookie terms: Once everyone decides you really *did* buy that cookie from that person for that much money, everyone officially writes down the purchase in his or her notebook . . . and you do, too.

STEP 4:
THE BLOCK IS ADDED
TO THE BLOCKCHAIN.

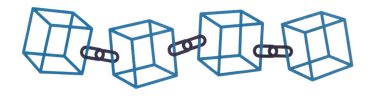

The block contains more than the records. It also is identified by its own unique code called a "hash." The block holding your record will also hold information about its hash—or code—as well as the hash of the previous block in the chain. These codes are what form the chain in a blockchain, and what connects the blocks together in the right order. If any information in the block changes, its hash changes, too, and so does the hash of the next block and the next. It has a domino effect that changes every block after that point in the chain. That's what makes the blockchain so secure.

Let the cookies explain. Everyone keeping a record of the bake sale now has a full page of sales records and binds the completed page into a finished notebook using a special superglue that makes it very, very difficult to change. If someone does try to change a record on a page in the book, every page in the notebook would change and not be usable anymore. Lucky for you, you don't have to worry about that. That's why Step 2 is important! You can just sit back, relax, and enjoy your cookie . . . finally!

BLOCKCHAIN OPPORTUNITIES

While Bitcoin popularized the blockchain technique of storing information, the blockchain can be used to store all kinds of data. Some say that blockchain technology is even more revolutionary than crypto-currency in its function as a distributed ledger that is very secure and difficult to corrupt. It may be able to help companies conduct business and verify information, identity, and ownership more quickly. It's also very secure, because once information is stored in the blockchain, it is almost impossible to make changes to it, which means it is difficult to hack. It may be helpful in any situation where trust is needed and hard to come by.

It can also help to streamline the process of tracking orders, payments, inventory (stock of an item in a warehouse), and more. This is because, traditionally, all of those processes were tracked individually by a variety of companies. Blockchain technology could make it so that the different groups could share a single distributed ledger protected by cryptography, which would make everyone both more reliable and more efficient.

THE BLOCKCHAIN MAY BE USED TO:

Help people track medical records more securely

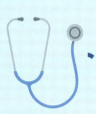

Make it easier to vote via computer securely

Allow people to own a share of a driverless car

Track crops and stop outbreaks of foodborne illness more quickly

60

Create digital books, music, movies, and other content that is almost impossible to copy, to allow creators to hold on to the rights and royalties

Track diamonds to ensure that the gems are ethically sourced

Prevent identity theft by making it harder to steal someone's online identity

CHAPTER 6

BIT BY BITCOIN

The first and possibly most well-known cryptocurrency is Bitcoin.

Bitcoin was invented in 2008 by Satoshi Naka-moto. Since the identity of the creator or creators are unknown, many people think Satoshi Nakamoto is a pseudonym, or a fake name, for a man, woman, or group of people.

Bitcoin was created to address some of the concerns people had with digital payments and credit cards.

LOL

Q: What do you call a coin with a bite taken out of it?

A: A bit coin

DIGITAL CASH

In a way, people wanted an online currency that would function more like cash, which is hard to track.

Cash has the advantage that no middleman needs to be involved in cash payments. Using cash to make a purchase only requires two people—the person buying and the person selling. To make a purchase with a credit or debit card or even a digital payment method, a third party is involved—the bank responsible for the digital payment or credit card, who often charges a fee to retailers, tracks purchases, and collects information on its users.

By removing the middleman, much of the concerns for privacy and collection of information is also removed. Imagine if you had a lemonade stand. To

make your lemonade, you bought lemons from a grocery store. That grocery store charges slightly more for each lemon than they paid the farmer the lemons came from, because one of the ways the grocery store makes a profit is by charging more than it paid for things. If you started buying lemons directly from that farmer, instead of from the grocery store, you would be cutting out the *lemon* middleman.

Now, imagine if that grocer had also been keeping track of all your purchases, and you didn't trust them to keep that information safe, you might be thrilled to have another place to buy lemons!

MINING:
HOW BITCOIN IS CREATED

Another way Bitcoin is different from the currencies that came before is by how it is created. Each Bitcoin is unique, created in a process called "mining." This isn't like the mining done to extract things from the earth. In fact, no hard hats are needed! That's because Bitcoins aren't actually mined by people at all. The mining is done by computers that are connected to a Bitcoin network over the internet.

To mine—or find—Bitcoin, people download software that allows their computer to join the Bitcoin network. When a computer is part of that network, it is called a "node." Then, when someone wants to buy, sell, or mine Bitcoin, the computers participating in mining help to process those transactions through a blockchain!

Next, the computers have to race one another to compete to solve cryptographic puzzles that are a bit like complex math problems. Why would they do this? Because the first computer to solve the puzzle gets a reward: brand-new Bitcoins!

The idea is that people (or their computers) are all working to help make the system function, and to confirm that Bitcoin transactions happening around the world are valid.

In the beginning, anyone with a computer could mine Bitcoin, but now it could take months because the math problems have become more complicated over time. But don't worry, there are other ways to buy Bitcoins, too!

HOW MANY BITCOINS ARE THERE?

Bitcoin is different than most currency in many ways, but one way Bitcoin is similar is that there is a limited amount of it. Only 21 million Bitcoins will ever be mined, and we are expected to mine the last Bitcoin by 2140.

BUYING BITCOIN

To purchase Bitcoins, or a fraction of a Bitcoin, that have already been mined, people can go to online markets called Bitcoin exchanges. However, since the price of Bitcoin is not stable, meaning that it goes up and down a lot, buying Bitcoin can be risky. The price of Bitcoin can change a lot at a moment's notice, while a more stable currency might only go up or down a tiny bit in a year. This matters because if someone buys Bitcoin for a high price one day and then the price of Bitcoin falls to a very low price overnight, their Bitcoin would suddenly be worth less than what they paid for it. This means that if the owner of that Bitcoin decided to sell it when the value was low, they would lose a lot of money. This is why it is best to wait to sell Bitcoin—or any investment, such as a house—until the value is high, and why many people lose money when they buy Bitcoin.

There are fun acronyms related to this: HODL stands for "Hold on for dear life" but originally started as a typo, or a spelling error, for the word "hold." It means that you should only buy Bitcoin if you can handle losing everything or are able to wait it out (hold on to your Bitcoin for dear life) until the price of Bitcoin goes up again after a crash so you don't lose all of your money.

Here's how it could work. If you went online and bought 10 dollars' worth of Bitcoin and the value of Bitcoin dropped overnight, the Bitcoin you bought could now only be worth one dollar. You could lose nine dollars in a matter of seconds! If you waited the days, months, or years it might take for Bitcoin to increase in value, you might eventually be able to sell it for 10 dollars again, or more.

WILL THIS BITCOIN FIT IN MY WALLET?

Instead of being stored in a physical wallet, Bitcoins are not actually stored anywhere. Instead, a software program called a Bitcoin wallet is more like a digital wallet that holds important information for Bitcoin owners. Since it is a digital wallet, it can be stored on a computer's desktop, an external hard drive, on a phone, or in the cloud.

WHAT'S IN *YOUR* BITCOIN WALLET?

One thing a Bitcoin wallet stores is something called a "private key" for each Bitcoin. It isn't like a metal key used to open the door to a house. It's a computer-generated code made up of a string of numbers. If you own Bitcoin, you need this key to access your Bitcoin and be able to spend it. It works like a secret code that helps owners find the Bitcoin address and which is needed to buy or sell Bitcoin. The thing is, if you lose this string of numbers, you also lose your Bitcoins!

A PERFECT PAIR

The private key is paired with a "public key," using complicated math to encrypt the data. The public key is also an encrypted, shorter version of a much longer number called a "public address" that is sort of like a home address for your Bitcoin wallet. If you are buying or selling Bitcoin, the public key helps point a buyer or seller to your wallet to add Bitcoins you buy from them or to remove Bitcoins you sell to them.

The way the private and public keys work together is called Public Key Cryptography and it is used to secure all kinds of data online, not just Bitcoin. The sender or seller of Bitcoin uses the private key to encrypt data and gives the public key to the intended recipient of that data. The recipient can then use the public key to decrypt the message to be able to read it.

BEYOND BITCOIN: ALTCOINS AND MORE!

Bitcoin isn't the only cryptocurrency out there. Most other cryptocurrencies are called Altcoins because they are similar to Bitcoin but with slight alterations. These are some of the strangest, funniest, and *cutest* cryptocurrencies.

DOGECOIN

This cryptocurrency began in 2013 and was inspired by a popular internet meme about a "doge" (an intentional misspelling of the word "dog"). The meme featured a photo of a Shiba Inu dog surrounded by colorful words expressing what the writer imagined were the dog's innermost thoughts in a quirky, dog-inspired English.

DENTACOIN

This cryptocurrency is made by dentists as a kind of token that can be used to help patients share dental records and materials more securely, and even to help patients pay for dental procedures. Maybe someday your dentist will accept Dentacoin to pay for braces!

WHOPPERCOIN

While only available at Burger King restaurants in Russia, Whoppercoin is a rewards program that uses the blockchain to encourage customers to return to stores to earn Whoppers. Yum! For each ruble (the basic unit of Russian currency) Burger King customers spend, they get one Whoppercoin. When they have 1,700 Whoppercoins, or about 30 US dollars, they get a free Whopper.

CRYPTOKITTIES

Cryptokitties aren't actually cryptocurrency! They are collectible unique illustrations of cats that can be used in a blockchain game and bought with a cryptocurrency called Ethereum. They can then be "bred" to create new Cryptokitties, which can be sold as well.

CRYPTO KIDS

Adults aren't the only ones giving Bitcoin a try; kids are investing in Bitcoin, too! While this all is very exciting, the price of cryptocurrency can change in an instant. It's possible these kids and other people who bought cryptocurrency were able to make money, but it's also possible that they could have lost that money later on.

So **do not try this at home** without your parent or guardian's permission and guidance, and when in doubt, only invest money that you are prepared to lose!

RAY RUSSELL

Age at first Bitcoin investment: 17 years old

Amount invested: $6,000

Amount purchased: Part of a Bitcoin, which were valued at $15,000 apiece at the time.

Result: In five months, after his original investment grew and he bought more Bitcoins, his investment grew to eight Bitcoins worth $70,000.

GEORGE WEIKSNER

Age at first Bitcoin investment: 11 years old

Amount invested: $200 he made by doing chores as part of his allowance

Results: His investment tripled in less than a year. He was lucky enough to notice the price of Bitcoin dropping and sold his just before the price crashed, or dropped from a very high to a very low price in a short period of time. He used the profits, or the amount he made on top of his initial $200 investment, to invest in a different cryptocurrency called Ethereum. He even started his own company—a cryptocurrency for gamers that he called a Pocketful of Quarters—with help from his father.

OZZIE WIMPFHEIMER

Age at first cryptocurrency investment: around 14 years old

Amount invested: $800, which was given to him by his parents. He invested it in another cryptocurrency called Litecoin. He liked that Litecoin only cost $180 apiece at the time, compared to Bitcoin, which was trading at around $10,000 apiece at the time.

Result: His investment doubled within two days!

THE GOOD, THE BAD, AND THE BITCOIN

Bitcoin is not perfect, by any means. It is great at certain things, but has some major downsides.

THE GOOD

Thanks to cryptography, Bitcoin may be safer and more secure to use for online purchases and is difficult to counterfeit (or make fake currency). It is also much faster and cheaper to send money to other countries compared to the traditional way, which could take days and charge high fees.

Another benefit to some people is that it's not backed by anyone. Instead, everyone who uses Bitcoin is also participating (or their computer is) in making sure it is accurate. It's sort of like the difference between a classroom where one person—usually the teacher—keeps track of homework and assignments and makes sure no one is cheating, and a classroom in which everyone, including the teacher and the students, is responsible for keeping track.

Cryptocurrency is also taxed differently than regular currency. Some people think of this as a good thing, but others don't like that it can take tax revenue away from the government. For example, if you were charged 10 percent tax on every purchase, and you made a $100 purchase, $10 of that money could be taken out to go toward paying for public schools.

THE NOT-SO-GOOD

While many people view the creation of cryptocurrency as a positive innovation for our society, there are also some downsides. One negative to cryptocurrency is that mining for new coins uses a lot of electricity—more each year than the whole country of Iceland—and is a big contributor to global warming. This is because to do all of those complex math problems, computers mining Bitcoin use a lot of energy!

It's hard to shop in the offline world with cryptocurrency, because it is not accepted in most shops and stores, and not even recognized as a legal form of money by many governments. Even if stores do accept Bitcoin or any cryptocurrency as payment, it currently takes longer and has more fees (to convert Bitcoin into local currency) than most other kinds of payments.

While cryptocurrency is also super safe, that can also be a bad thing! It can be a target for hackers. Even though it is very secure in some ways, some Bitcoin exchanges have been hacked and people have lost their money. Bitcoin wallets stored on computer desktops, phones, and on the web have been hacked, too. In addition to hackers, the fact that it's not as easily tracked can make it easier for people to buy illegal products or participate in illegal activity.

Another part of cryptocurrency that keeps it secure but could also be seen as a flaw is the fact that if the hard drive where your Bitcoins are stored crashes, or you forget your private key, you lose all of your Bitcoins. Forever! People who bought Bitcoin early on when it was cheaper can make a lot of money if they sell it when Bitcoin is valued at a higher price, but some of them lost their private key or keys and can't claim their Bitcoins! That's a mistake you wouldn't make twice . . .

Cryptocurrency is still in its early days. We're still learning about how it will change the world, for better or for worse. What do you think will happen? Do you think it's a good thing, a bad thing, or something in between?

CHAPTER 7

?

WHAT'S NEXT?

With cryptocurrency, mobile money, digital payment options, and more, it's hard to know what the money of the future will be like. Maybe cryptocurrency will take off and everyone will use it. Maybe it will be something more people use, but only a portion of the population. Or maybe someday countries will replace their national currencies with cryptocurrency—or something that hasn't been invented yet! Some people predict that a quarter of the world's national currencies could be replaced by cryptocurrency in just a few years.

LOL

Q: Which kind of nut makes the best money?

A: A cashew!

DIGITAL DOLLARS, OR EVEN A UNIVERSAL CURRENCY?

There are even predictions that there will be a digital version of the US dollar someday . . . one that uses the blockchain so that the government can keep track of where the money is going. It's possible . . . but will it happen? Only time will tell!

There could even be a universal currency that is used across the world, in the same way that the euro became the currency for twelve countries in 2002, replacing national currencies like the franc in France, the lira in Italy, and many more.

VIRTUAL PURCHASES?

Maybe there will be new ways to make purchases. There's speculation that in the near future, people might be able to use virtual reality headsets to shop. They'll *feel* like they're shopping at a store—even if they're actually at home, or any-where!—and even be able to make purchases while they browse the virtual aisles!

FAREWELL TO PENNIES, NICKELS, CREDIT CARDS, AND CASH?

There have been arguments over the years that the US government should stop making pennies, in part because pennies cost more to make than they are worth! The reason for this is because coins last much longer than paper bills, and the old bills are shredded and sent to landfills, creating waste.

What if all physical money were no longer used? Can you imagine a world where all currency was more valuable as confetti or flooring than as payment?

Or, if cryptocurrency—or any other digital currency—replaces the world's currencies someday, what do you think would happen with all of the coins and bills, and even credit cards?

CASH CONFETTI AND *ACTUAL* MONEY BAGS?

Maybe you would use cash in a new way. When the currency in Venezuela lost its value, people started to use the nearly worthless cash as a *material* instead of as a form of payment. They wove paper money into bracelets and baskets and shredded money to make confetti.

Maybe you could make a dress out of dollar bills. After all, they are made of cotton and linen!

PENNY FLOOR TILES?

If pennies go out of production, they might make a great flooring. Since US pennies have a relatively low value, some people already do this. It's affordable, and it makes the floors look pretty cool!

Whatever happens, the future of money probably looks different than anything we can imagine. Even 100 years ago, people probably didn't think we would use tiny handheld computers, known today as smartphones, to magically send money to one another! What do you think money and financial transactions will be like in another 20 or 50 years? What about 100 or 500 years?

Will crypto be king? Will wind power be so valuable that people use it to make purchases? Will dollars and cents be a thing of the past? The only certainty, it seems, is that it will look different from anything we could have imagined, and might be used in different ways, too. Maybe you will be the one who comes up with the next big innovation!

WRITE YOUR COIN NAME ABOVE